This book is given with love from

_____

to

_____

Digger's Tale
The Story of the
Hero Dog

Copyright © 2024 by KiCam Projects

All rights reserved. No part of this publication may be reproduced, stored in a retrieval system, or transmitted, in any form or by any means, electronic, mechanical, photocopying, recording, or otherwise, without the prior written permission of the publisher.

Cover and book design by Lucia Benito

ISBN 978-1-7345642-7-3

Printed in the United States of America

Published by KiCam Projects

www.KiCamProjects.com

Dedicated to
our hero dog, **Digger**.

Your paw prints left
an imprint on our hearts.

We love you!

Digger was a good dog,
he was everyone's best friend.
He took really good care of us
right to the end.

He was a special part
of our family,
everyone would say,
he even saved a life
one tragic day.

When **Digger** was young
he loved playing outside,
he never could dig
a big enough hole,
but boy would he try.

Digger slowed down
as he got a little older.
He stopped playing outside,
especially when it was colder.

At the end of **Digger**'s life,
it was hard to say goodbye,
but he found his place in heaven
and once again,
he's playing outside.

Losing a member
of your family
is a hard thing to do,
but it's a part of life.
It's sad but it's true.

Even though Digger is gone,
he's never far away.
He lives forever in our hearts,
each and every day.

About the Author

Kilee Brookbank Kersteff is an inspirational author, speaker, animal lover – and burn survivor. Severely injured when a gas leak caused her house to explode in November 2014, Kilee was hospitalized for thirty-eight days before returning home to a life of new challenges and a new "normal." Kilee wrote the award-winning Beautiful Scars: A Life Redefined and is the founder of the Kilee Gives Back Foundation. Her inspiring story has been featured by The Doctors, Inside Edition, MTV, Seventeen, Girls' Life, Woman's World, and Redbook.

Explore other Digger
(and his fur-siblings) inspired books at
kicamprojects.com

Digger the Hero Dog

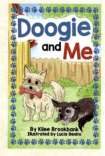

Doogie and Me

Our New Friend Dori

Our Toys Are for Sharing

Enough Love for All

About Digger

Digger lived a happy and full life with his family – fur and human. His legacy will live on through his books, helping to educate children on the importance of fire safety and teaching valuable life lessons.